# My Learning Adventures

# 1 2 3

**Silver Dolphin**

San Diego, California

1 1 1 1 1

one one

1

Find the correct sticker and place it here.

1

one

# Count the objects in each group. Color the box with one object.

Turn to page 79 for the answer.

# 2

2 2 2 2

two two

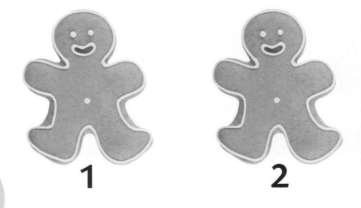

1      2

**Find the correct sticker and place it here.**

2

two

Use the stickers in the front of the book to add 2 beach balls, 2 pails, 2 boats, and 2 seashells.

# 3

3 3 3 3

three three

1     2     3

Find the correct sticker
and place it here.

3

three

6

# Count the objects in each group. Circle the groups of three.

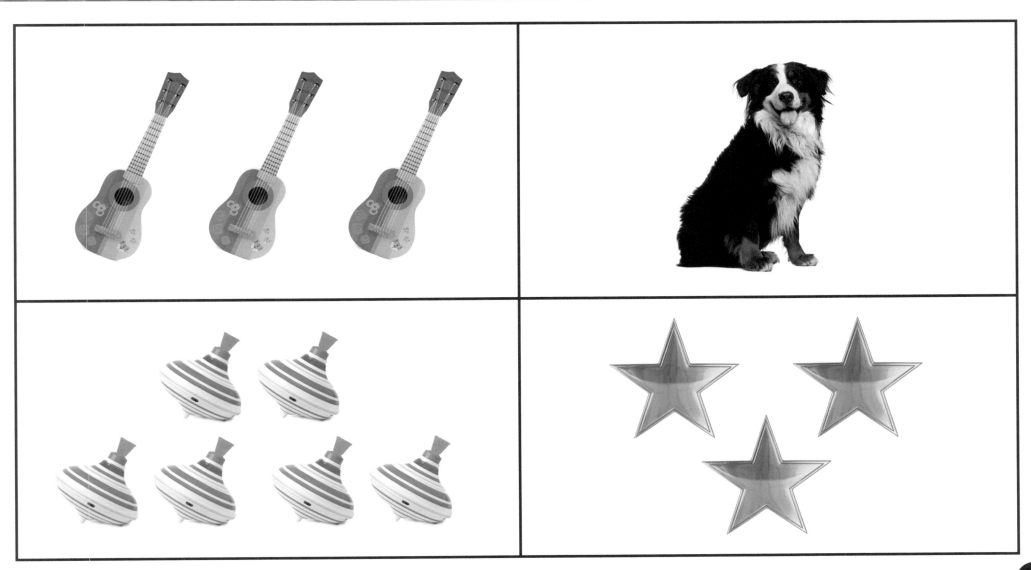

Turn to page 79 for the answer.

# 4

4 4 4 4

four four

1     2     3     4

Find the correct sticker and place it here.

4

four

8

# Count the objects in each group. Color the groups of four.

Turn to page 79 for the answer.

**Trace the number 5 and the word five.**

5 5 5 5

five five

1    2    3    4    5

**Find the correct sticker and place it here.**

5

five

# Count the objects in each group.
## Match the number to the group with the same number of objects.

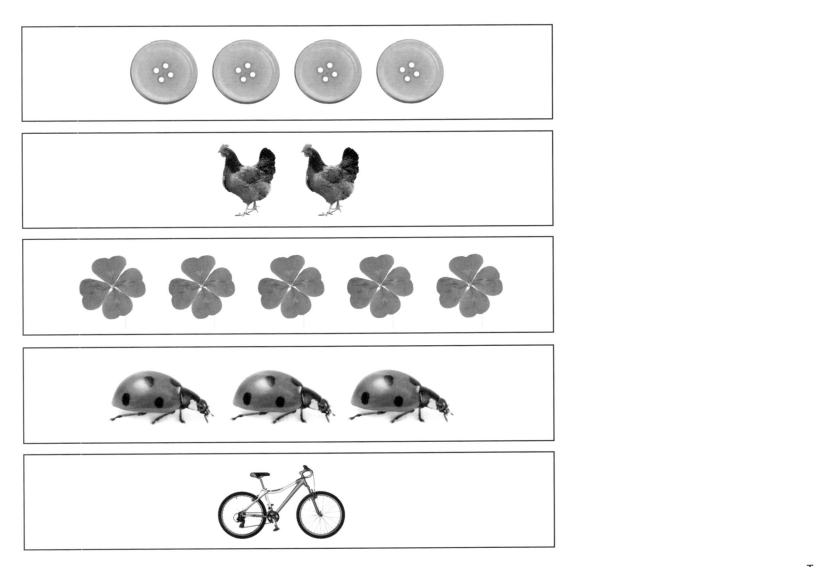

Turn to page 79 for the answer.

# 6

6   6   6   6

six   six

1    2    3    4    5    6

Find the correct sticker and place it here.

6

six

12

# Count the objects in each group. Circle the group of six.

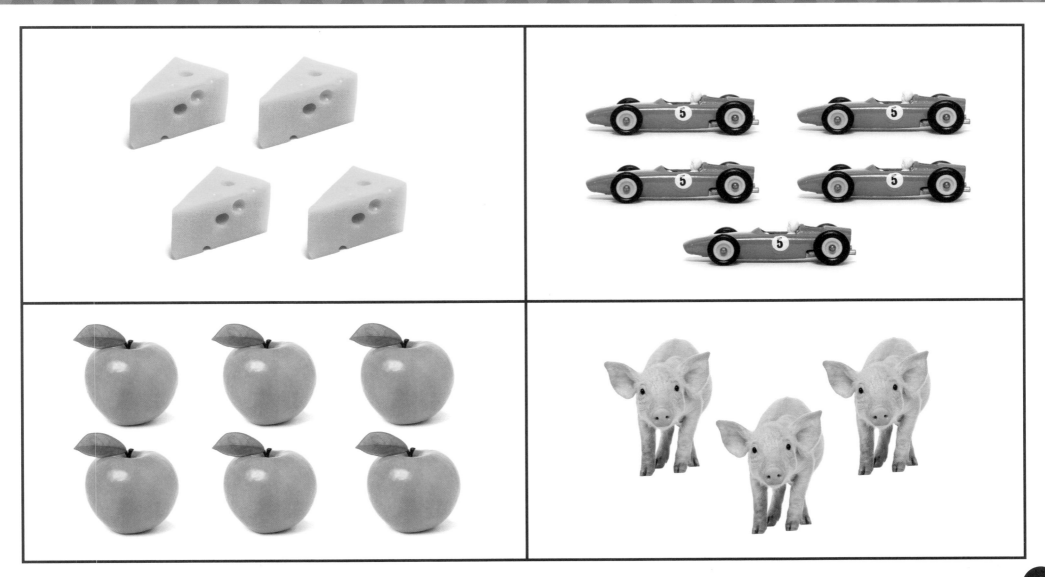

Turn to page 79 for the answer.

# 7 Trace the number 7 and the word seven.

7 7 7 7

seven seven

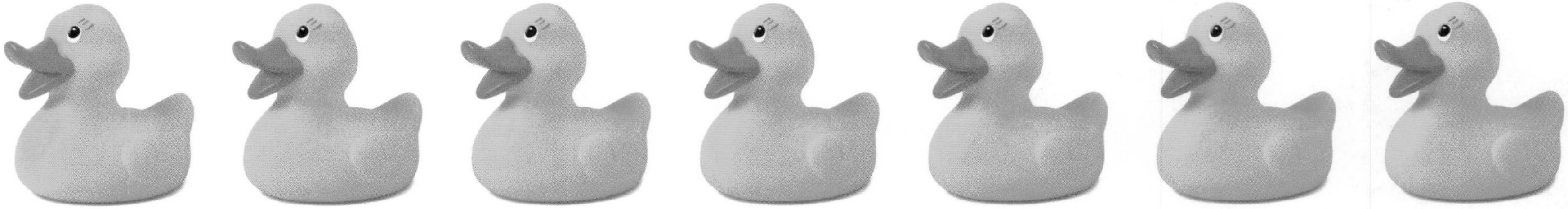

1 2 3 4 5 6 7

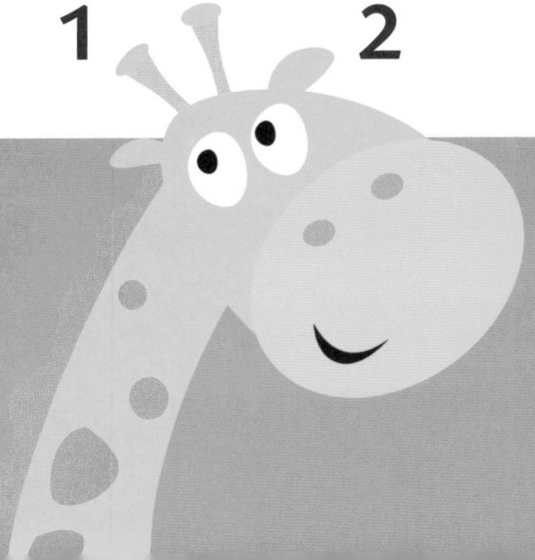

**Find the correct sticker and place it here.**

7

seven

# 8

8 8 8 8

eight eight

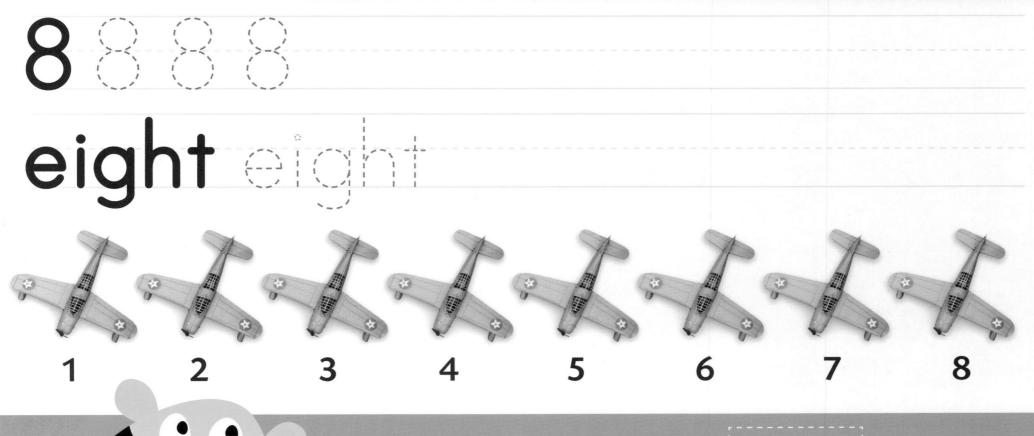

1    2    3    4    5    6    7    8

Find the correct sticker and place it here.

eight

16

# Count the objects in each group. Circle the groups of eight.

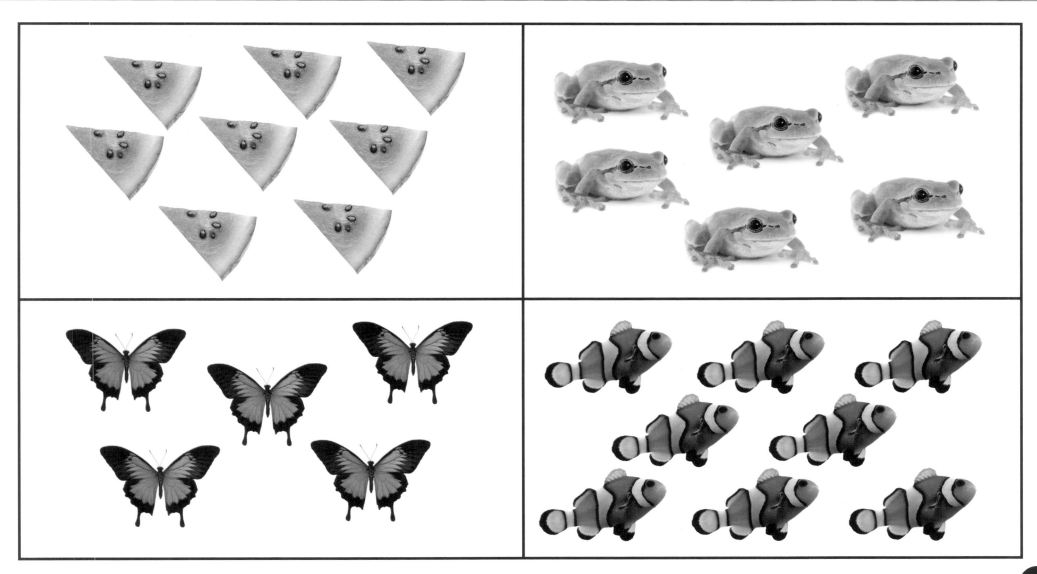

Turn to page 79 for the answer.

# 9

9 9 9 9

nine nine

1    2    3    4    5    6    7    8    9

Find the correct sticker and place it here.

9

nine

18

# Count the objects in each group. Color the groups of nine.

Turn to page 79 for the answer.

**Trace the number 10 and the word ten.**

10 10 10 10

ten ten

1    2    3    4    5    6    7    8    9    10

**Find the correct sticker and place it here.**

10

ten

# Count the objects in each group.
## Match the number to the group with the same number of objects.

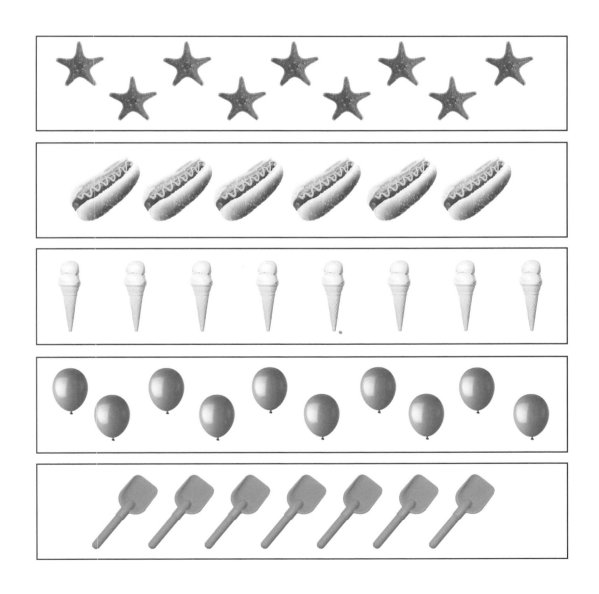

6

10

7

9

8

Turn to page 79 for the answers.

# Little Fish: To the River!

Fry, Flo, Flip, Fan, and Fin are the last little fish in their nest. All of their brothers and sisters swam off in search of food. But the little fish are scared. What if they get lost?

"Come on! Come meet all of my turtle, crab, and frog friends!" said their big sister Flitter.
"Are there scary creatures in the river?" asked Fin.
"We'll be safe if we stay together," Flitter answered. "Let's try!" cried Fry.
He swam out into the rushing river.

Punch out the fish in the front of the book. Place them on the page to count along with the story.

= 1

**One little fish in the river.**

"This is fun!" said Fry. "Okay. I'll go!" cried Flo. She glided over to join Fry.

**Two little fish in the river.**
"Yay! Let's take a trip!" cried Flip. He waded into the river.

**Three little fish in the river.**

"I can do it! I know I can!" cried Fan.
She drifted over to Fry, Flo, and Flip.

+ + + = 4

Four little fish in the river.

"Come on, Fin! It's fun!" cried Fry, Flo, Flip, and Fan.
Fin was scared that his brothers and
sisters might leave without him.
"Count me in!" cried Fin. He plunged into
the rushing river and they all began
to swim down the river.

+ + + + = 5

**Five little fish in the river.**

Punch out the pennies in the front of the book. Read the number in each price tag. Place the correct number of pennies next to each price tag.

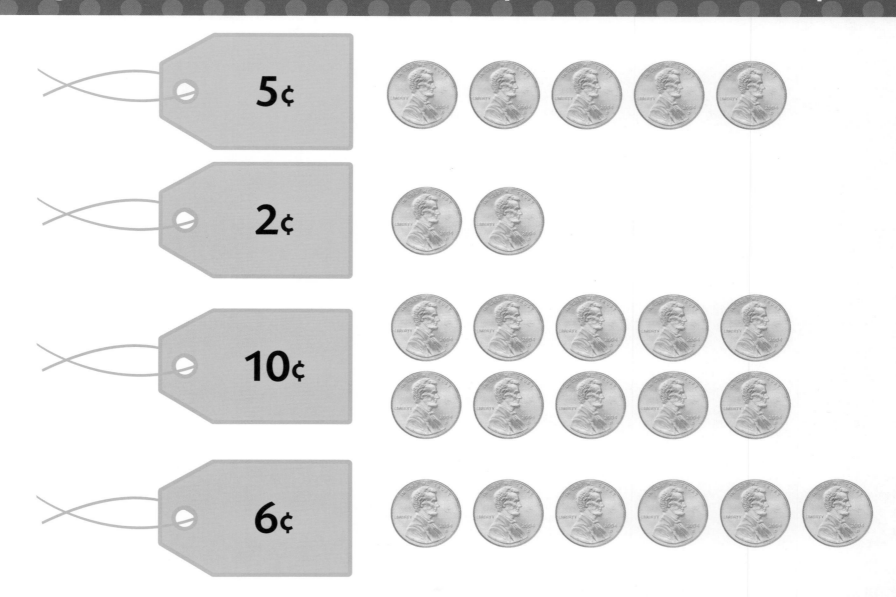

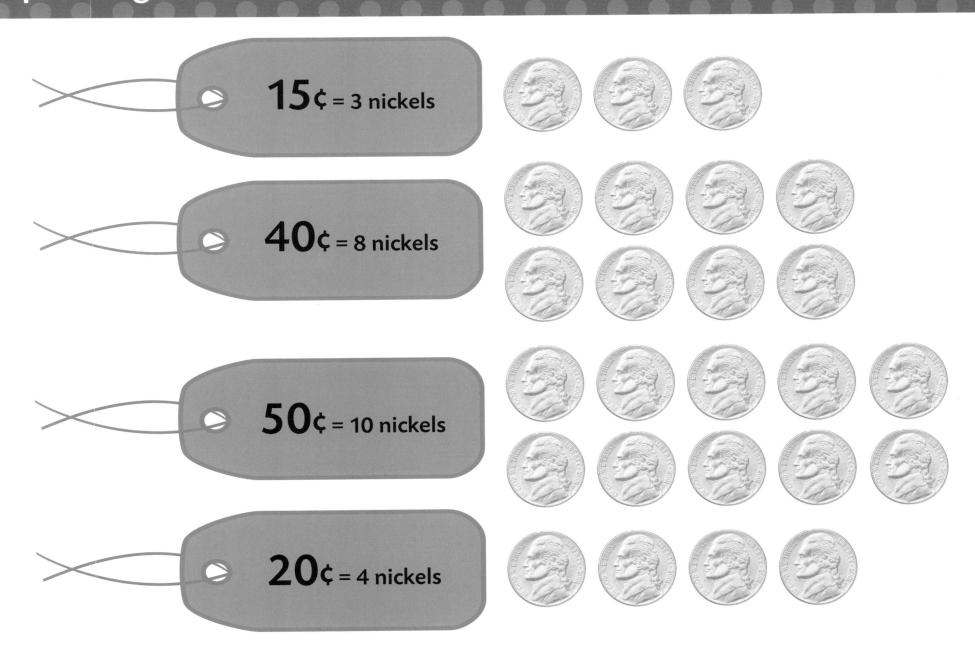

15¢ = 3 nickels

40¢ = 8 nickels

50¢ = 10 nickels

20¢ = 4 nickels

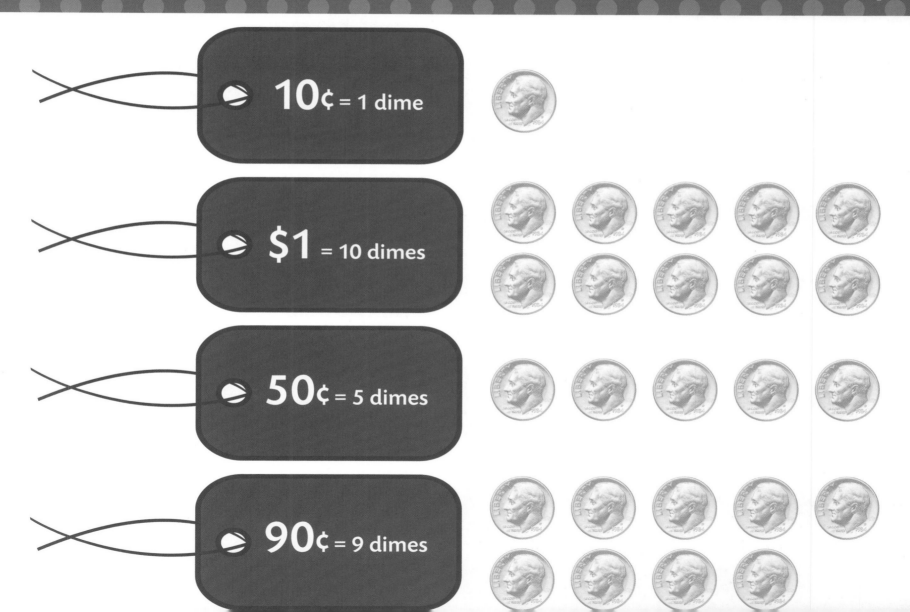

10¢ = 1 dime

$1 = 10 dimes

50¢ = 5 dimes

90¢ = 9 dimes

**5¢ = 5 pennies or 1 nickel**

**10¢ = 10 pennies or 2 nickels or 1 dime**

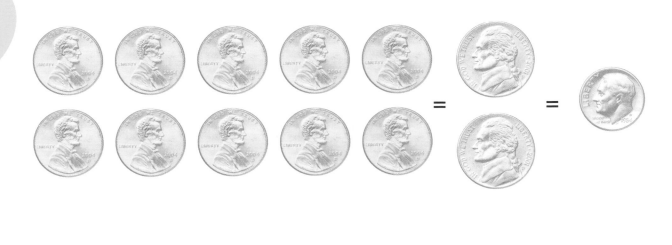

29

# Telling Time

A clock has two hands.

The little hand points to the hours and the big hand points to the minutes. Each smaller line is equal to one minute. Write the time below each clock.

**9 : 00**

__ : ____

__ : ____

__ : ____

__ : ____

Turn to page 79 for the answers.

# Draw lines to match the clocks with the time that they show.

2:00

5:30

11:15

8:05

Turn to page 79 for the answers.

# Read the time below each clock.
## Draw a little hand on each clock to match.

1:00

4:10

7:35

11:50

Turn to page 79 for the answers.

# Read the time below each clock.
## Draw a big hand on each clock to match.

**1:00**  **12:15**  **5:30**  **11:45**

Turn to page 79 for the answers.

# Little Fish: To the Sea!

**Punch out the fish in the front of the book. Place them on the page to count along with the story.**

Fry, Flo, Flip, Fan, and Fin have traveled down the whole river! On their river adventure, they met Tammy the turtle, Craig the crab, and Flounce the frog. But all of their brothers and sisters have swum out to sea. Now that Fry, Flo, Flip, Fan, and Fin are not so little anymore, it is time for them to head to the sea too.

**Five little fish in the river.**

"Come on! Come meet my dolphin, whale,
and lobster friends!" said their big sister Flitter.
"But there are big, scary monsters in the sea!" said Fin.
"We'll be safe if we stay together," Flitter answered.
"I'll try!" cried Fry. He swam out into the deep blue sea.

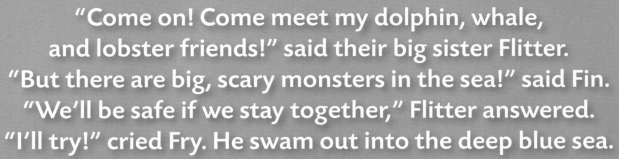

**Four little fish in the river.**

"Wow! This is great!" said Fry. "Let's go!" cried Flo. She floated out to join Fry.

**Three little fish in the river.**

"Okay. Let's take a dip!" cried Flip. He dove into the sea.

**Two little fish in the river.**

"We can do it! I know we can!" cried Fan. She waded out to Fry, Flo, and Flip.

**One little fish in the river.**

"Come on, Fin! It's fun!" cried Fry, Flo, Flip, and Fan. Fin was a brave little fish. He was ready to join his brothers and sisters.

"Count me in!" cried Fin. He rushed out to the sea and together they set off on a new ocean adventure.

**Zero little fish in the river.**

# Counting Fingers

How many fingers are there? Circle the correct number.

5
9
2
1

6
9
7
4

4
6
8
5

3
7
10
4

Turn to page 79 for the answers.

# Count the kittens in each basket. Write the number in the box.

**kittens**

**kitten**

**kittens**

**kittens**

Turn to page 79 for the answers.

# Someone forgot to put the buttons on these coats. Finish the coats by drawing on the correct number of buttons.

4 buttons

6 buttons

3 buttons

Turn to page 79 for the answers.

# Count the number of flowers in the scene.
# Write the number in the box.

flowers

Turn to page 79 for the answer.

41

# Count the bugs in each row.
# Write the number in the box.

Turn to page 79 for the answers.

# Count the number of apples in the trees. Write the number in the box.

apples

Turn to page 79 for the answer.

# Draw the correct number of goldfish in the fishbowls.

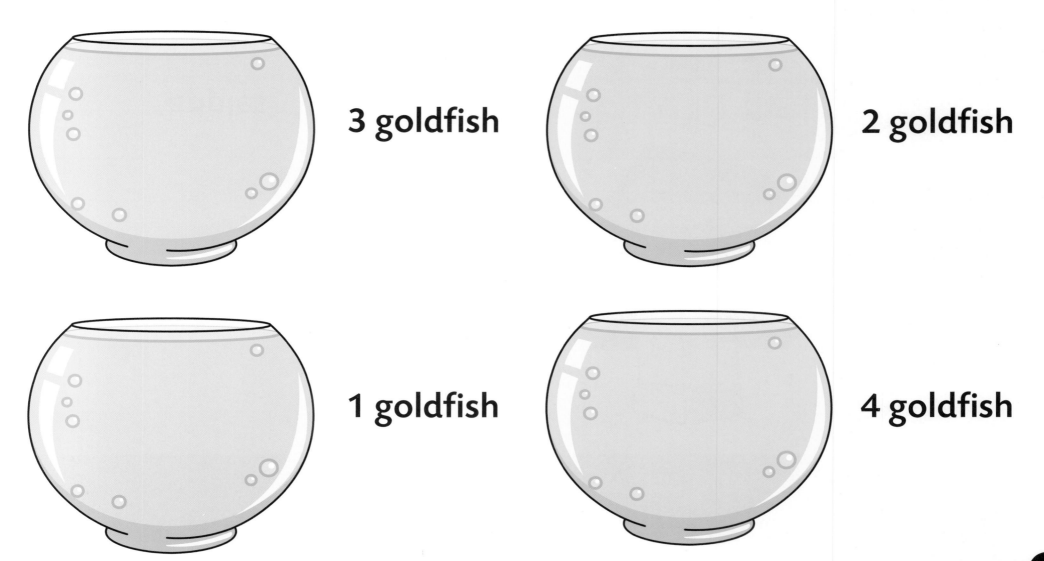

3 goldfish

2 goldfish

1 goldfish

4 goldfish

Turn to page 79 for the answers.

# Draw 6 stars in the space scene.

# Count the items listed below.
# Write the number next to each item.

_____

_____

_____

Turn to page 79 for the answers.

# Circle the cake in each row that has the fewest candles.

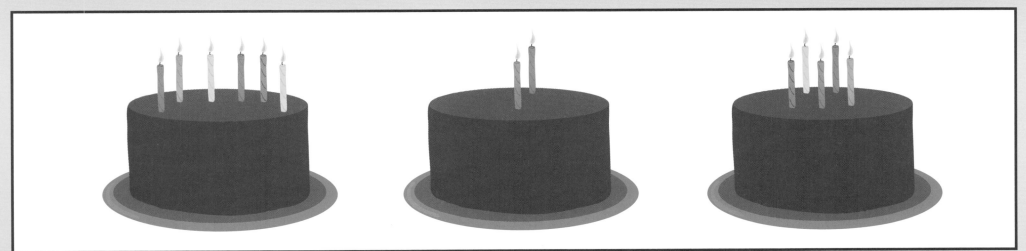

Turn to page 80 for the answers.

# Count the spots on the ladybugs.
# Draw a line from the ladybug to the correct word.

one          two          three          four          five

Turn to page 80 for the answer.

# Count the crayons.
## Draw a line from the crayons to the correct word.

six

seven

eight

nine

ten

Turn to page 80 for the answer.

# Fill in the missing numbers.

Turn to page 80 for the answers.

# Fill in the missing numbers.

1    ☐    3

☐    5    6    7    ☐

# Draw a line from the number to the correct word.

one          two          three          four          five

Turn to page 80 for the answer.

# Draw a line from the number to the correct word.

9  7  10  6  8

six        seven        eight        nine        ten

Turn to page 80 for the answer.

# Circle the group in each box that has the fewer number of objects.

Turn to page 80 for the answers.

# Circle the group in each box that has the greater number of objects.

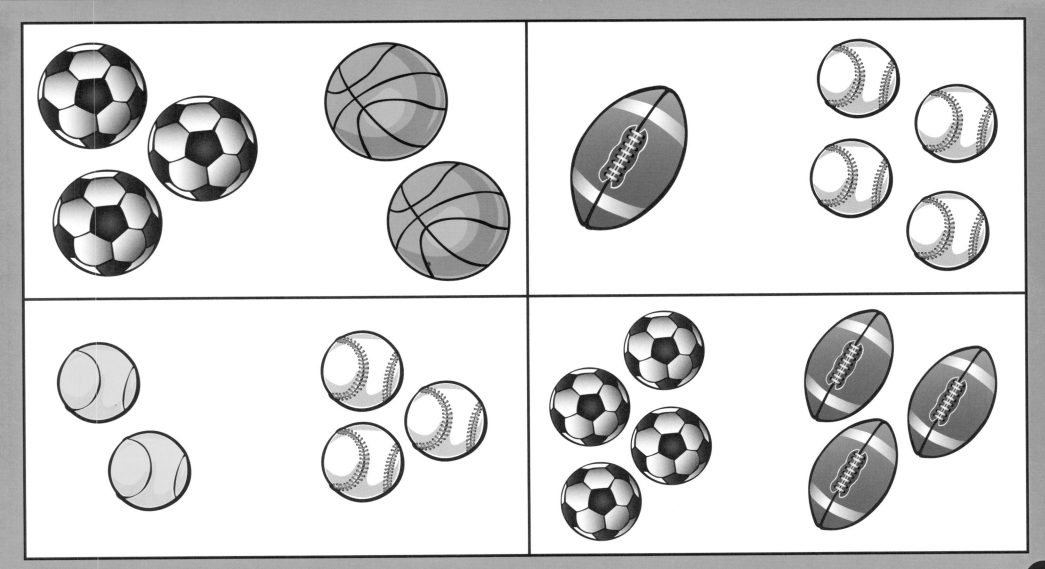

Turn to page 80 for the answers.

# Circle

**Circles are round.**

**Trace a circle.**

**Draw a circle.**

**Name the round objects.**

Find the correct sticker and place it here.

circle

# Color in all the circles.

Turn to page 80 for the answer.

# Oval  Ovals look like eggs.

**Trace an oval.**

**Draw an oval.**

**Name the oval objects.**

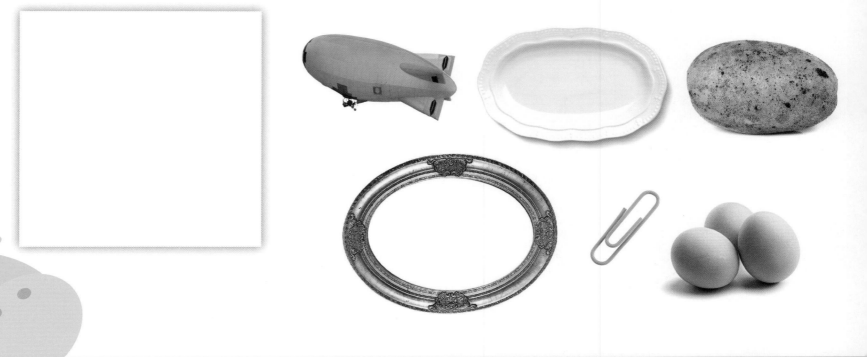

# Help this bird collect his eggs and return them to the nest. Color the ovals to create a path to get there.

Turn to page 80 for the answer.

# Square

**Squares have four equal sides.**

Trace a square.

Draw a square.

Name the square objects.

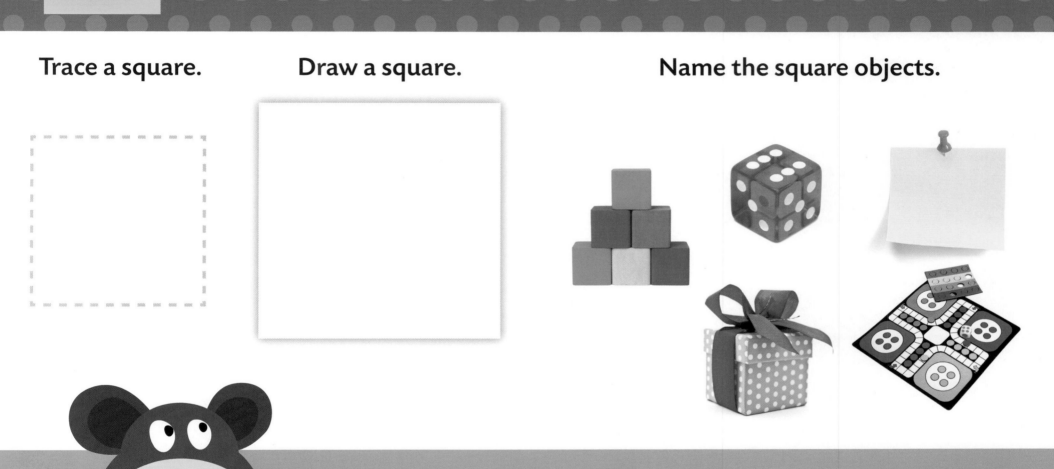

Find the correct sticker and place it here.

square

# Help the truck make a delivery to the house in the maze.

Turn to page 80 for the answer.

# Rectangle

A rectangle has four sides. Two sides are long and two sides are short.

**Trace a rectangle.**

**Draw a rectangle.**

**Name the rectangular objects.**

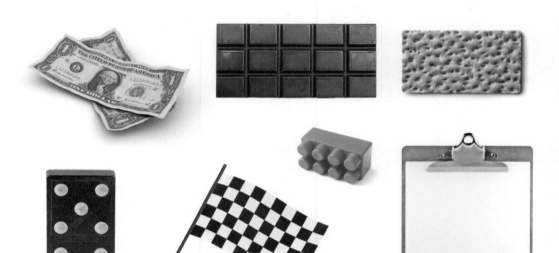

**Find the correct sticker and place it here.**

rectangle

# Color in all the rectangles.

Turn to page 80 for the answer.

# Triangle Triangles have three sides.

**Trace a triangle.**

**Draw a triangle.**

**Name the triangular objects.**

Find the correct sticker
and place it here.

triangle

# Color in all the triangles.

Turn to page 80 for the answer.

65

# Diamond

A diamond has four sides.
Diamonds stand on one corner.

**Trace a diamond.**

**Draw a diamond.**

**Name the diamond-shaped objects.**

**Find the correct sticker
and place it here.**

**diamond**

# Circle all the diamonds.

Turn to page 80 for the answer.

 # Heart

Hearts have two curves at the top and come to a point at the bottom.

**Trace a heart.**

**Draw a heart.**

**Name the heart-shaped objects.**

UR MINE

**Find the correct sticker and place it here.**

heart

68

# Help the puppies find their mom!

Turn to page 80 for the answer.

# Star

**A star is a shape with 5 points and 10 sides.**

**Trace a star.**

**Draw a star.**

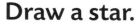

**Name the star-shaped objects.**

**Find the correct sticker and place it here.**

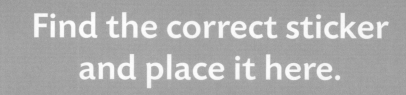

star

# Connect the dots to complete the starfish picture.

There are many different shapes at a playground. Use the stickers from the front of the book to create a fun scene.

# Color the two shapes that are alike.

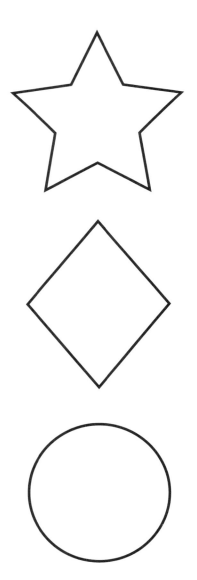

Turn to page 80 for the answer.

# Color the shapes in each row that are alike.

Turn to page 80 for the answer.

# Circle the shapes that are the same size in each group.

# Help this puppy fetch all the balls and put them in the basket. Color the circles to create a path to get there.

Turn to page 80 for the answer.

# Count the number of circles on the teddy bear's bed. Write the answer in the box.

circles

Turn to page 80 for the answer.

# Use the shape stickers in the front of the book to make some crazy creatures.

# Answer Key

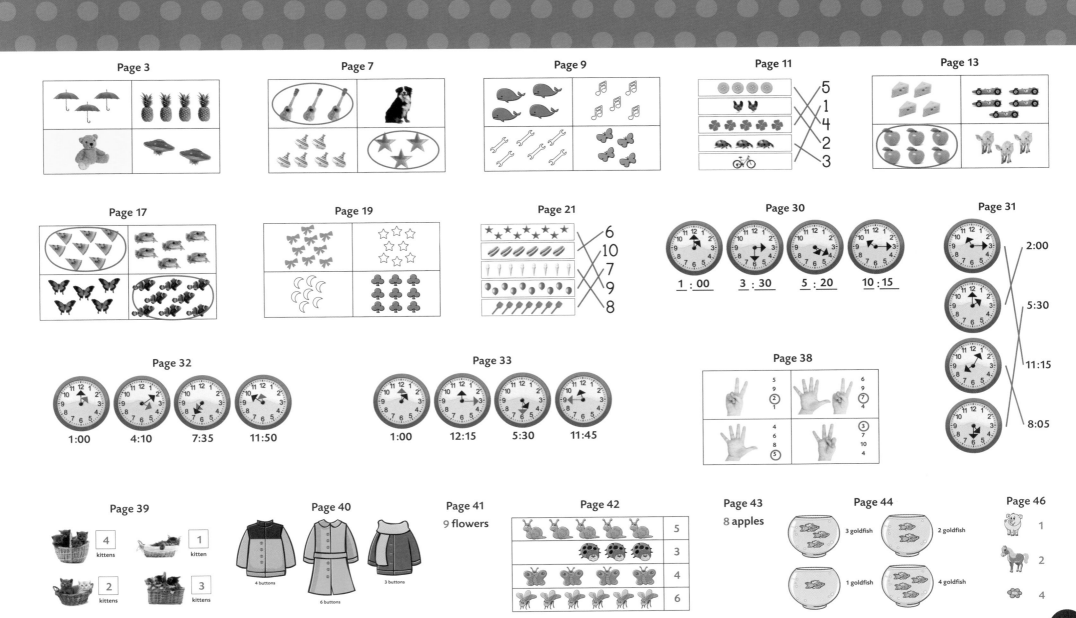

79

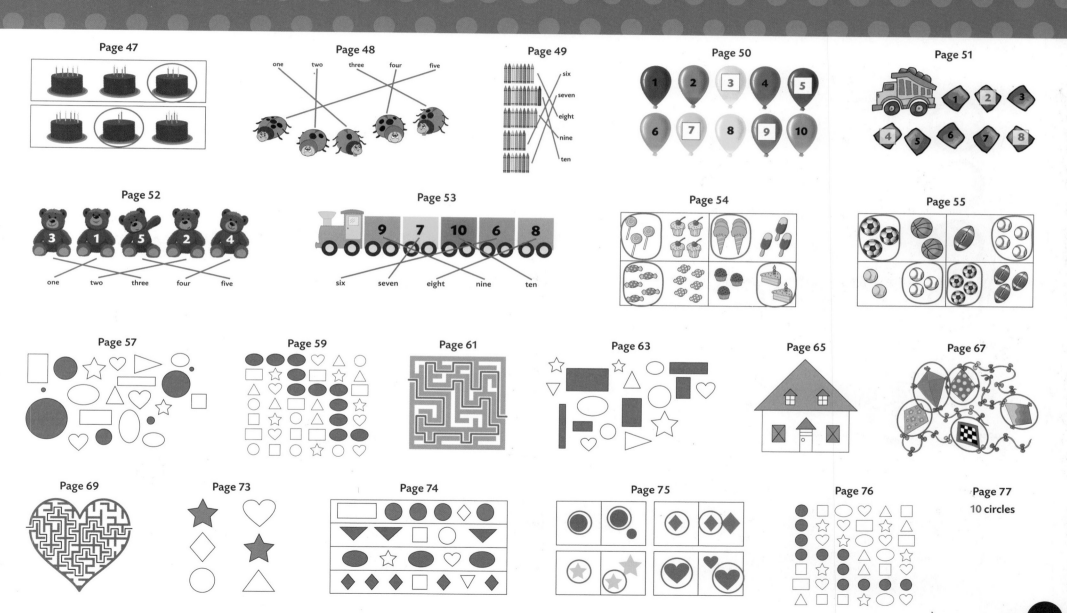